The Word of God That Penetrates the Heart of Mankind

New Improvement

Rev. Dr. Burness W. Freeman

ISBN 979-8-88751-046-0 (paperback)
ISBN 979-8-88751-047-7 (digital)

Christian Faith Publishing
832 Park Avenue
Meadville, PA 16335
www.christianfaithpublishing.com

All scriptures, unless otherwise stated, are taken from the King James Version of the Holy Bible.

Printed in the United States of America

CONTENTS

INTRODUCTION

I have always prayed and asked God to help me be a light. I wanted first to be a light to my family, and God has done that for me.

Since I became close to God, I learned to orchestrate my life in a way of trying to lead others to God.

My whole life has changed since I opened the door of my heart and let Jesus come in.

I got saved at the Pee Dee Union Baptist Church in Cheraw, South Carolina, where I started my first job in the church as an usher. God called me to preach one year after joining the Usher Board.

In 1968, I preached my first sermon at the Pee Dee Union Baptist Church in Cheraw, South Carolina. My first churches were the Nicey Baptist Church in Jefferson, South Carolina; New Zion Baptist Church in Chesterfield, South Carolina; and Mt. Rona Baptist Church in Society Hills, South Carolina.

God blessed me eight years later to pastor the St. John Missionary Baptist Church in Latta, South Carolina.

Four years later, I moved to Bright Light Baptist Church in Lancaster, South Carolina. God has been using me to build up His churches.

I was the pastor of Timmonsville Baptist Church in Chesterfield, South Carolina. Since 1993, I have been the pastor at the St. Matthew Baptist Church in Bethune, South Carolina.

God has helped me to serve all these churches, and I left each of them in a peaceful way.

God has blessed me to serve as Moderator of the St. Paul Union in Chesterfield County. I also served as President of the Bright Light Missionary and Education Convention, in Lancaster, South

Carolina. Additionally, I served as Vice Moderator and Moderator of the St. John River Union, Lee County.

I retired from Wachovia Bank, and I have furthered my education at Shaw University in Raleigh, North Carolina (2004).

I love golfing and bowling.

Somehow, I always find time to travel as a Delegate each year to the National Baptist Convention in the United States.

God has blessed me to enjoy a great family, pastor great churches, and travel to great conventions. I have had a great life. I thank God for a wonderful life, and I love people.

An Ungrateful Generation

Text

> Give thanks unto the Father, which hath made us meet to be partakers of the inheritance of the saints in light. Who has delivered us from the power of darkness, and hath translated us into the kingdom of his dear Son. (Colossians 1:12–13)

Theme: An ungrateful generation

God can bless some people with an overflow of goods, but they don't know how to be thankful. God is always worthy of the adoration of His own people. Thanksgiving is an expression of gratitude; it is a national holiday set apart for giving thanks to God and is celebrated on the fourth Thursday of November in the United States. On the second Monday of October, in Canada, they celebrate Thanksgiving. The people of this country didn't show any thanks to the ones who tried to help us. They didn't show enough to go out to vote. Some didn't thank the president for fighting for health care; some didn't thank them for lowing credit card rates, reforming Wall Street, and fighting for the middle class. We are an ungrateful generation.

People are too obscure to deal with, and in other words, they are too hard to understand. I cannot understand how people can vote for someone who got them in the mess in the first place. Some people don't know their enemies from their friends. Where is common sense? All the Republican Party wants to do is fight for the rich, and that fight seems to be relentless. They also want to castigate the president instead of being thankful for his hard work.

The president can't have an ascertain mind when most of the country let him down. He has been put in an implicit way of life, but God is still in charge. It is hard to be explicit without the voters' support. People should be thankful when people try to help them. There's one thing for which you should be abundantly thankful for—God's grace. It shouldn't be what you have in your pocket that makes you thankful, but it's what you have in your heart. It is always something to be thankful for. We should be thankful to be on this side of the grave.

If you don't have anything to be thankful for, you need to check yourselves. Your job may be harder than you would like for it to be, but still, be thankful you have a job. We can be thankful for the bad things we don't have to deal with and enjoy the good things that God has blessed us with because it could be the other way around. A person doesn't realize how much he has to be thankful for until he loses it. We may not get all we want, but we should be thankful for what we have. We should give thanks for all the bad things God didn't let come our way.

God is our help in times of trouble. We all have a lot to be thankful for. Even as bad as this country we are living in, we should be thankful for America. We have come a long way in this country; I don't believe God brought us this far to leave this unthankful generation. We can even be thankful for some of our so-called friends we no longer have. We should wake up with thanksgiving in our hearts every morning.

Prayer is the key to getting God's attention. We can reach God through prayer. Prayer and walking on the wrong side of the road don't go together. You can't live any kind of way and get a prayer through. It was said, "God hears the prayer of the righteous, but the unrighteous is far off."

Every day should be Thanksgiving. My Thanksgiving is being able to get up this morning.

The Mystery of God

Text

> But we speak the wisdom of God in a mystery, even the hidden wisdom, which God ordained before the world unto our glory. (1 Corinthians 2:7)

> But, beloved, be not ignorant of this one thing, that one day is with the Lord as a thousand years, and a thousand years as one day. (2 Peter 3:8)

Theme: The mystery of God

The word *mystery*, as used in the Scriptures, refers to something, which was not known in the past but is now revealed. Our Lord used it when He said, "Because it is given unto you to know the mysteries of the kingdom of heaven." In 1 Corinthians 2:9, "But as it is written, eye hath not seen, nor ear heard, neither have entered into the heart of man, the things which God hath prepared for them that love Him."

Man feels he knows, but we don't understand anything about God if He doesn't reveal it to us. We have some folks who want to know too much too quick. God is the only One who knows it all. We look at one day as twenty-four hours, but God looks at one day as a thousand years. There is a big difference between man's thinking and God's thinking. We have some folks seventeen to nineteen and some older folks who think they know everything. If the truth is told, they know much of nothing.

Let's look at what 2 Peter 3:8 says, "A thousand years in God's sight, but as a day." In man's sight, it is only twenty-four hours a day, but in a day, it is a thousand years in God's sight. We look at it as twenty-four hours, but in God's day, it is a tenth of God's time in a day of twenty-four hours—which would be fifteen minutes. It's a hundred years of our time, but in God's time, it would be two hours and forty minutes.

In God's sight, mankind hasn't lived a whole day. In man's sight, if you reach one hundred, you will be two-hour and forty-minute old in God's day! It has been told that at seventeen, you have only lived a tenth in God's day. We have too many sayings. I don't want to hear what folks have to say and haven't lived a day in what God calls a day. God is the only one who knows it all, but sometimes, some folks think they know at all. We don't sometimes know it, but sometimes, we don't know if we are right of wrong. Our best is like filth rags in the sight of God. We can't make ourselves look good enough to get into God's kingdom. It took a mystery from God. The blood of Jesus is the only plan that God put together for man's salvation.

Mankind thinks they have a plan for salvation. Some folks try to tell you that eating hog meat is a sin, but adultery is not. It is not what goes in the body but what comes out of you. It is those evil things that come out of you. One thing I know is that I want a savior who not only died but also got up from the grave. I do know Christianity is built on a live prophet and not on a dead one. One thing I do know is that we have a God who is able to lift us from where we are to a better tomorrow. We are serving a God saying, "Knock, and the door shall be opened."

God is a mystery all by Himself. He is our triumphant savior. Christianity is not about retaliation but repentance. We are serving a God of mystery, and all good gifts come from Him. It is a mystery how God can get one thousand years from one day, and we can only get twenty-four hours. Jesus is our mystery: He is the very nature of God. He is the very character of God. He is the very sustenance of God. He is the very perfection of God. He is God in all of His perfect being. Jesus may not be the same person as God the Father, but He has the same perfect nature. He is God the Son. Therefore, the mystery is that the person who has seen Jesus Christ has seen the Father in all the fullness of the Father's nature.

"Eye hath not seen, nor ear heard, neither have entered into the heart of man." In 1 Corinthians 15:51,

> Behold, I show you a mystery: we shall not all sleep, but we shall all be changed. The Bible goes on to say: we will be changed in a moment, in the twinkling of an eye, at the last trump. This is a Mystery of God: "For the trumpet shall sound, and the dead shall be raised incorruptible, and we shall be changed."

The Lord Himself shall descend from heaven with a shout, with the voice of the archangel, and with the trump of God.

God Has a Strange Way of Sending Missionaries

Text

> Therefore they that were scattered abroad
> went everywhere preaching the word. (Acts 8:4)

Theme: A mission that seems impossible

God turned loose the enemy on the missionaries who were in Jerusalem in order for them to spread the word of Jesus Christ. We try to fit God into our purpose, but we need to wait until God fits us in His purpose. The book of Acts records the beginning of the church or the birth of the church. The book of Genesis records the origin of the physical universe. The book of Acts records the origin of the spiritual body, which we designate as the church. God gave His missionaries the tools they needed to get His work done; they all were filled with the Holy Ghost.

A spiritual gift is a special attribute given by the Holy Ghost to every member of the body of Christ. A true missionary can't help from having concern for others. Missionaries should be concerned about people in a foreign land and at home. We have some living in this country who don't know the Lord. How can we be concerned about folks at home when we don't know Jesus? The missionaries at Jerusalem had love in their hearts, and they were willing to die for what they believed. The missionaries in Jerusalem were prosecuted because the devil wanted to destroy the church before it got started.

God has a way of doing things that man can't understand, but that was God's way of moving the church out of Jerusalem so that others would hear His word. God fixed a way for the missionaries to follow its full commission, which was to spread the word of Jesus. After all Saul did to God's church, the Lord graciously blessed him and decided not to kill Saul but to save him. Because of what Saul did, the church accomplished what Jesus had ordered the church to carry out. God uses different methods to bring us to the point of recognizing His power. God used a method to scatter His church so the unbelievers could hear the preaching of Jesus Christ.

We need some true missionaries because the churches seem to have left off sound teaching and sound doctrine. Paul said, "In the last days; people would depart from sound preaching, and teaching." If we want to see Jesus, we must hold to God's hand, build our hope on eternal things, and hold to God's unchanging hands. God's true missionaries have been anointed to teach and preach sound doctrine. The Spirit of the Lord is upon those missionaries He sent to heal the brokenhearted. God used them to recover the sight of the blind and to set liberty for those who are bruised. God's church has struggled with depicting and defining itself as the light of her Lord. Missionaries on the move have been sent by God since God didn't call us to set down but to turn the world upside down.

God has a strange way of sending out His missionaries.

The Walk That Pleases God

Text

> Blessed is the man that walketh not in the counsel of the ungodly, nor standeth in the way of sinners, nor sitteth in the seat of the scornful. (Psalm 1:1)

Theme: A walk that pleases God

Our text tells us how God's children should walk. We must walk like we are looking forward to that day when we shall be caught up to meet the Lord in the air. If we are to make it to that city, we need to walk in a way that pleases God. We must walk in ways that please God because that day will come so suddenly and unexpectedly until it will be too late for us to get ready. A day of terrible destruction and pain will come, and it's a day of no escape if we aren't walking to please God.

If we live in God's will and walk in righteous, we should have that blessed assurance one day. If we die in Christ, at His dramatic appearance, the saints will be with Him when He returns. The Lord's return is to comfort and edify believers who please God in their walk. How can we please God? It's by growing in His prefect love and living a good life.

We must learn to mind our own business and work out our own soul's salvation. We shouldn't worry so much about pleasing mankind, but we must do all we can to please our God. Psalm 1:1 says, "Blessed is the man that walketh not in the counsel of the ungodly, nor standeth in the way of sinners, nor sitteth in the seat of the scornful."

We should be like a tree planted by the rivers of water. If our walk pleases God, we should not be followers of everything that comes along. If our walk pleases God, we will not be like the chaff that the wind drives in all directions. If our walk doesn't please God, we can't stand in the congregation of the righteous. God knows the thoughts of our hearts.

Spiritual Dead Zone

Text

> And ye shall know that I am the Lord, when I have opened your graves, O my people, and brought you up out of your grave, And shall put my spirit in you, and ye shall live, and I shall place you in your own land: then shall ye know that I the Lord have spoken it, and performed it, saith the Lord. (Ezekiel 37:13–14)

Theme: A spiritual dead zone

For some folks, it doesn't matter what you do or what God does, they're not going to hear you. God gave His people a land flowing with milk and honey, but they wouldn't hear God's voice. He told them they were not to have any other gods before Him. He gave them laws, statuses, commandments, and standards, but they broke them. After God was so good to His chosen people, they hit some spiritual dead zones. They became thoughtless, disobedient, stiff-necked, and determined to pursue their own way of life. They started to make changes.

They turned to a god who couldn't do anything for them, and they left God who could do everything for them. The dead zone of prosperity caused them to forsake God who has the power to make the sun rise and go down. They neglected the worship service and deserted God. God tried to help them in their prosperity, but they failed to hear Him. God spoke through His preachers, but they failed to obey His voice (Jeremiah 22:21).

God warned Israel of her sins. If she will turn from her ways, He will not turn away His punishment (Amos 1:3, 6, 9, 11, 13). Proverbs 6:19 said, "Israel became false witnesses and they sowed discord among the people." God had gotten down to His last straw. I feel like God is down to His last straw with the people of this world and with things like same-sex marriage, lies, and hatred.

We see where God had chosen Israel to be a witness, but instead, they forsaken Him (Deuteronomy 4:23). He said to Israel, "In the day that you forget me I will call heaven and earth to witness against you" in Deuteronomy 4:26. God warned them, "When you stop worshipping me and start running after gods made with men's hands, wood, stone, silver, and gold, I will scatter you among the nations." Deep grief had driven them to the riverbanks in Babylon. When they were carried down in Babylon, they were able to hear God.

When folks get in trouble, they talk to God and hear Him. We sometimes don't miss our water until the well runs dry. They wept when they remembered Zion. They sat in silence; they remembered in silence; they wept in silence. God had to bring them down to get their attention; after they lost their civil liberty and after they lost their religious liberty, they heard God. We sometimes have to hit a dead zone before we hear God. Out of all God has done for us, we just turn around and slap Him in the face. We have moved God from our daily prayer life, and this world is pushing for same-sex marriage, God forbid.

We have too many church folks who feel like the world, think like the world, and act like the world. The Lord said, "The day you hear my voice harden not your heart." He is saying to us, "Come unto me all ye that are heavily laden, and I will give you rest." If you are in a spiritual dead zone, the Lord is saying, "Behold I stand at the door and knock; if any man will open I will come in and sit down with you."

The Lord will get you out of your spiritual dead zone.

God Is My Refuge

Text

> God is our refuge and strength, a very present help in trouble. (Psalm 46:1)

Theme: You are in good hands

Sometimes we think we are alone, but God has us in His hands in times of trouble. Trouble is hard to work around; it has no respect of person, and trouble doesn't discriminate. It has a way of plaguing the black man, and it also has a way of plaguing the white man. It plagues the young people; it plagues grandpa and grandma. Trouble also plagues the learned and the unlearned. Trouble will find its way through prayer; it has a way of breaking through the walls of prayer; but if God is before you, it will not have any power.

If you have not had an encounter with trouble, just keep on living. We need to prepare for trouble just like we prepare our meals each day. There is a word from the Lord in Psalm 46:1, "God is our refuge in time of trouble." God is the only one who has the power to keep trouble from coming our way. We don't know how much trouble would have come our way if God had not turned it in another direction. God is able to divert trouble in a different situation and send the storm that is in our lives in another direction. Some of our lives would have been a disaster if God had not calmed the storms in our lives.

God has a way of moving when His people are in trouble. He cleared a path through the Red Sea for His people. God sent the wind to dry the ground of the Red Sea, and His people's shoes didn't get muddy as they marched through the sea. Daniel was also in trouble. We need to put him on the stand and hear what he has to say about God being a refuge. I feel he would say, "They tried to stop me from praying, and I was thrown into the den of hungry lions. God was my refuge in times of trouble."

"God is our refuge and strength, a very present help in trouble" (Psalm 46:1). You are in good hands when you are in God's hands. Through all Job's troubles, God was his refuge. Job's flesh had started to rot away from his bones, but God was his refuge and strength. Job was in good hands.

God is our refuge and strength. It has only been through the grace of God that we as blacks survive the trouble times we have gone through. We were in good hands—in God's hands.

When It Seems Like Everything Is Lost

Text

> Then Job arose and rent his mantle, and shaved his head, and fell down upon the ground, and worshipped, And said, naked came I out of my mother's womb, and naked shall I return thither: the Lord gave, and the Lord hath taken away; blessed be the name of the Lord. In all this, Job sinned not, nor charged God foolishly. (Job 1:20–22)

Theme: When it seems like everything is lost

When Job thought that all was well, it turned out to be his worst day. It is bad when you lose all your earthly possessions in one day, but it is worst when you lose Jesus. The Bible said that he went to the secret place of the Most High God, fell down on his knees, and said, "Naked came I out of my mother's womb and naked shall I return."

Through it all, Job still wanted to bless the name of the Lord even though his prosperity was turned into adversity. God let Satan touch Job, but He put a restriction and limitation on Satan. He let Satan touch the part of Job that was made of earth but not his soul. It's the part that one day the undertaker will bury—the remains. He told him he can touch the part of the skin that worms will destroy but not mess with the soul.

Now, Satan, you can touch the part that one will lay on the cooling board and a winning sheet. You can touch the part where the blue waters of death will settle in his eyes; his finger nails will turn purple. The 206 bones in our bodies will be chilled, and our tongue will cleave to the roof of our mouth. God didn't care if Satan touched the part of Job that one day would be hauled away in a hearse and buried six feet in the earth.

Job didn't let Satan pull him over. No man can say he is in God's presence and does Satan's dirty work. Job didn't give into Satan even though he was a victim of a disease. It was said, "Satan blew into his nostril and a poison heat immediately turned his blood into corruption so that his whole body became an ulcer." But through it all, Job maintained his integrity with God, and through it all, Job kept in touch with God.

He also had three friends: Eliphaz, Bildad, and Zophar. It was said, "For seven days they sat in eloquent silence and sympathy alongside of Job on his ash pile." Job said, "Why did I not die from the womb?" After Job had cursed the day that he was born, this gave way for Job's friends to probe into his private life.

They accused Job of having committed some secret sin. Job sat there knowing that he had done no wrong. One of the worst feelings in the world is to be accused of something, and you know you didn't do anything. Job had to roll with the punches. You have to watch your best friends. The condition that causes the turmoil in our world is caused by people letting Satan use them. Plagues come from human filth, fire starts from human carelessness, and wars come from human hate and greed.

Job didn't blame God for his suffering. It is totally unfair to God when some people try to blame Him for their sufferings and inconveniences when God made everything good, and man messed it up. Count it all joy even when you fall into the diver's temptation.

The thing that is more important than our philosophical speculation about trouble is that when we do suffer and have our troubles, it gives us the chance to see what God can do. When it seems like all is gone, God will step in when we need Him the most. Is there anything too hard for God?

In the midst of adversity, God will deliver you. God can take our adversities and use them in His master plan. We don't know why Job had to suffer like he did. I don't understand how God created the heavens and earth. I don't understand how a black cow can eat green grass, give off white milk, and churn yellow butter. I don't understand how you can put a seed in the ground and it grows food. I don't understand how a sea of water can be turned into a dusty path or road. I don't understand how God could fireproof a fire furnish. Job couldn't understand how all these things could happen to him, but he believed that nothing was too hard for the Lord.

Job was trying to find God, but all he had to do was just look at the trees. Heaven declares the glory of God, and the earth shows forth his handiwork. If he had just smelled the perfume that came from the rosebud, he would have seen God's glory. Job should never question God's wisdom. He asked Job, "Where were you when the Morning stars sang together, and all the sons of God shouted for joy" (Job 38:7).

Christ Is the Head of
the Church Family

Text

> For whosoever shall do the will of my Father which is in heaven, the same is my brother, and sister, and mother. (Matthew 12:50)

> For the husband is the head of the wife, even as Christ is the head of the church: and He is the Savior of the body. (Ephesians 5:23)

Theme: Christ the head of the Christian family

The body of believers, known as the church, is also referred to as the "household of God." Don't trust in a friend; don't put your confidence in a companion. We must learn to put our trust in the one who is the head of the Christian family. Our elders seek to teach us, direct us, and keep us on the path of righteousness; often, we don't hear them until it's too late.

As Christians, we embrace the legacy of our families, but even more, we need to embrace the legacy of Jesus Christ, the head of the Christian family. We must strive to emulate Jesus in every way and hold to the standards that He has set for us in His written word. His written word leads us on the trail to lift the lives of the lost. His written word leads us to the old rugged cross. Jesus told His disciples that a true friend sticks closer than a brother. A true friend is one who is willing to lay down his life for a friend. Mankind didn't elect Jesus to be the head of the Christian family; the Father appointed Him to be the head of the Christian family. He was appointed head of the church family: He makes intercession with the Father for His church family.

Jesus is our heavenly advocate, He is a prayer-answering God. He hears and acts when we pray. In Romans 8:28, "He makes all things work together for His Christian Family's good." He is gone away to prepare an eternal dwelling place for the Christian family. The Christian family has a true friend in high places, making intercession and bearing the mark of His crucifixion. Jesus is our friend in high places. We can boldly ask God with the expectation that our request will be answered. The master of the Christian family has made a way for us to draw near with confidence to the throne of grace.

When we drop our heads in despair, Jesus, the head of the Christian family, will dry our weeping eyes. When we feel abandoned, Jesus, the head of the Christian family, promises never to leave us—never to leave us alone. Jesus is our greatest friend who shows us His greatest love by bearing the old rugged cross. He was wounded for all of our transgressions, and He was bruised for our iniquity! He died for our sins, but He didn't stay dead. When the *sun came up*, the *Son got up* from the grave with all power.

The head of the church family is there for His family members who have become victims of alcohol and drugs. He is there for the incarcerated family members—those who are spiritually lost. Jesus, the head of the Christian family, is there for the young and the restless, who are standing on the edge of the night and going through their secret storms. Jesus, the head of the Christian family, can make the impossible possible: He has the power to give hope to the hopeless! He is able to raise up your bowed down heads. He can turn bitter defeat into victory. Jesus is the head of the Christian family: He gave His life for His family!

If you are down and out, you can give Him your despair, and He will give you hope! Give Jesus your sorrow, and He will give you joy. Give Him your negatives, and He will give you His positives! Give Jesus your sickness, and He will give you health. Jesus is the head of the Christian family. We can give Him our confusion, and He will give us peace of mind. He is able to replace hatred with love. Jesus is a friend you can depend on twenty-four seven.

If you are weak, He will give you strength. If you trust in Him, Jesus will take your doubts and give you faith. He will take your bondage and give you freedom. He will take your arrogance and give you humility. He is our hope for tomorrow.

Graduation Day

Text

> For promotion cometh neither from the east, nor from the west, nor from the south. But God is the judge: he putteth down one, and setteth up another. (Psalm 75:6–7)

Theme: Graduation day

Mother Burch knew her graduation day was approaching. She knew it was time to put her mind around the challenges of the future. She put her hands on the tasks in front of her and her heart in the direction she was going. She was getting ready for her graduation day, and it was time for her promotion.

She enrolled in the school of hard knocks of life many years ago, but the other day, she graduated and joined the clouds of witness. God has promoted Mother Burch from eternal sorrow to eternal joy. He has promoted her from eternal damnation to eternal grace and mercy. She has been promoted and not demoted. She has been promoted from eternal condemnation to eternal justification.

Mother Burch saw the dark shadow of her homegoing approaching. She knew the time of her departure was at hand, and she was ready for her promotion. She was ready for her graduation day, and she had completed all of her life courses.

There are some courses we can't afford to drop, and that is the course of salvation. Mother Burch has passed her final test, and she has gotten her homegoing assignment. Everyone who got to know Mother Burch has been touched by her love, and she had so much love for her family. She will always be in my memory. She was a lady who stood on the promises of the Lord, but God put her on His graduation list.

She gave up the ghost, and He gave her eternal life. Mother Burch gave Jesus her despair, and He gave her eternal glory. She gave Him her sorrow, and He gave her His joy. She gave Him her sickness, and He gave her an eternal and glorious body. Mother Burch wouldn't want you to be sad at her transition. She is with the graduates. John said, "Couldn't be number."

In Mother Burch's sick hours, she was surrounded by darkness, but morning came, and it was graduation season. Morning has come into her life, and there will be no more sleepless nights. Weeping may endure for a night, but joy comes in the morning. On graduation day, joy came, and Mother Burch got her third degree: Father, Son, and Holy Ghost. In her life, she traveled toward the east seeking light because she knew graduation season was approaching, and when it was all over, she just wanted to say, "Good morning, Jesus."

The promotions and blessings we receive in this life come from the Lord. This Psalm is a song of deliverance, and we must look to God for our promotion. This Psalm is telling us that our help didn't come from the east nor from the west nor from the south, and it didn't mention the north because that is the direction the enemy came from, but only God is able to deliver His people and promote them. We must trust God; stand on the promises of the Lord; and if we stand on His promise, one glad morning when this life is over, we will fly away.

The Triangle Presentation of God

Text

> And Jesus, when he was baptized, went up straightway out of the water: and, lo, the heavens were opened unto him, and he saw the Spirit of God descending like a dove, and lighting upon him: And lo a voice from heaven, saying This is my beloved Son, in whom I am well pleased. (Matthew 3:16:17)

Theme: The triangle presentation of God

A triangle means a situation involving three persons: the eternal triangle—the Father, Son, and Holy Ghost. Jesus ascends from the water of baptism, the Holy Spirit descends from heaven in the visible form of a dove; the Father spoke from heaven, saying, "This is my beloved Son, in whom I am well please." The three persons are in evidence at one time at the baptism of Jesus. All the persons of the Trinity are coequal and coeternal.

The Greek word *monogenes* means the same. If the triangle presentation of God is in your life, it will help you to withstand the storms of life. The reason some of our churches are going through so many storms is that the triangle presentation of God is not present.

We have fine church building going up, but nobody was coming to Jesus; we have our covered dish suppers and big churches, but no souls are being saved.

The triangle presentation of God needs to be present for God's church to catch on fire. God can't do anything for folks when they turn against Him. He is standing at somebody's door knocking this morning. We have too many blind folks trying to run God's churches. I think a lot of Little Stevie Wonder, but I am not going to let him drive my car. The devil is using church folks to shed darkness on his church service while others are trying to shed light.

When we are faced with the storms of life, we need to trust God and hold onto His unchanging hand. We must trust God when the doctor gives a bad report because no matter how heavy the load is, the triangle presentation of God will help you lift your load. In life, we all sometimes have to carry heavy loads, but trust in God's power, not yours. When groceries get low and when the phone is being disconnected, God is there. When heavy loads are on our backs, we must pray like Jesus. He took His eyes off the people and lifted His eyes and prayed. Sometimes, to go to the other level, you have to take your eyes off the people and put them on God. It is hard to serve God looking at people; there comes a time when you have to look around people to see Jesus.

Jesus is the sinner's savior and the giver. He is Noah's ark, Abraham's ram, Jacob's stone, Moses's law, David's shepherd, Solomon's rose of Sharon, Ezekiel's wheel, Daniel's stone, Isaiah's comforter, Jeremiah's battle ax, Malachi's promise of blessing, Matthew's king, Mark's healer, Luke's Son of God, John's word made flesh dwelling among mankind, Peter's rock, Paul's sufficient grace, and Jude's deliverer. According to Revelation, "He is King of kings and Lord of lords." He was connected with the triangle presentation of God.

Early one Sunday, when the sun came up, the Son got up with all power in His hands. If you are connected with the triangle presentation of God, you shall rise again, and death can't keep you in the ground. You will join the cloud of witnesses and have a great family reunion in heaven. He was connected with the triangle presentation of God.

In Revelation 1:18 Jesus said, "I am he that liveth, and was dead; and behold, I am alive for evermore, Amen; and have the key of hell and of death." Early one Sunday, when the sun came up, the Son got up with all power in His hands. If you are connected with the Triangle Presentation of God you shall rise again and death can't keep you in the ground. You will join the cloud of witnesses and have a great family reunion in glory.

When a Man Fails God

Text

And Adam knew Eve his wife; and she conceived, and bare Cain, and said, "I have gotten a man from the Lord."

And Cain talked with Abel his brother: and it came to pass, when they were in the field, that Cain rose up against Abel his brother, and slew him. (Genesis 4:1 and 8)

Theme: When a man fails God

We have about 41,100,000 black men in this country, and about 919,000 are in colleges and about 827,680 in prisons. Crime begins with the man Cain, the son of the first earthly father Adam. Abel's blood is placed alongside Christ's shed blood, which is better than Abel's in that Abel's blood cried out for vengeance, but the blood of Christ cries out for mercy. Abel's blood, although the blood of a righteous man, cannot atone, but Christ's blood is every efficacious.

Abel is unique among men in the Bible in a fourfold direction. Abel was the first man of the human race to die; he was the first man on earth to be murdered. We have prisons that are almost filled with murderers, but God needs men to make their lives living sacrifices. Abel was the first saint to present an offering acceptable to God.

Cain was the eldest son of Adam, the first man to be born, but he failed God. The terrible story of Cain proves how quickly man's fallen nature developed. It did not take long for Cain's heart to become desperately wicked, and the line of Cain continued in sin. Man will let jealously get the best of him. Cain's heart became jealous as he witnessed the happiness of his brother Abel and his favor with God. Ultimately, he yielded to jealous feelings and killed his brother Abel.

We must have the right attitude for the reception of God's gift. Man doesn't have to fail. He must believe in the incredible and wait for the inevitable. God has promised to lead His people; we can claim what God has promised us and receive what God wants to give us. We must keep looking up to God, reach out for the intangible, and look up for the invisible. God needs men who are willing to fight the unbeatable foe and achieve the impossible dream.

Man doesn't have to fail when serving an all-powerful God: Jehovah-Jireh is our great provided. Jehovah-Elohim is our redeemer. Man doesn't have to fail (Genesis 2:4). Jehovah-Rapha is a healer, and He is able to heal our land (Exodus 15:26). He is Jehovah-Nissi: In Exodus 17:15, "The Lord is our banner of victory in battle."

Man doesn't have to fail with God on his side. He is Jehovah-Shalom: When you have a troubled heart, He will give you peace. When Cain's heart got troubled, he should have looked to Jehovah-Shalom for peace.

Making a Personal Decision

Text

> And Saul asked counsel of God, "Shall I
> go down after the Philistines? Will thou deliver
> them into the hand of Israel?" But he answered
> him not that day. (1 Samuel 14:37)

Theme: A personal decision with divine guidance

Making the right decision depends on our destiny. We look at decisions as an act or a process of deciding—a determination. It also means to arrive at after consideration. Our decisions have a lot to do with our destiny. It is our decision alone that can make our life happy or unhappy. There will be some who will encourage you to make the right decision, and there will be others who will try to make a personal decision for you, but a personal decision should be made by that person.

Our destiny is at stake in every difficult decision we make in life. Honest or deceitful or brave or cowardly or kind or cruel or responsible and unreliable, our decisions count. We can be good person but make bad decisions; they can cost us dearly. We can be very talented, and we can have good looks, but that will not get us anywhere when we make bad decisions.

Our achievements depend on how we make decisions. A person can accomplish what he or she wants in life just by using the God-given sense granted to that person. A person's character can carry him a long ways; we all are going to have some deficiencies in life, but rightful thinking will enable us to overcome our deficiencies. We must make the right decision in pursuing a career because we have some folks who think they know more about what is best for us. We have folks who will try to lead us down the wrong career path. Sometimes, you have to make your own personal decision.

In Psalm 32:8–9, "I will instruct you and teach you in the way you should go; I will counsel you and watch over you. Do not be like the horse or the mule, which have no understanding but must be controlled by bit and bridle or they will not come to you." We must learn to make decisions through God's guidance.

As we pursue God and seek to trust Him as our Lord, He promises to lead us. God has not created us to be controlled like an animal. Some folks try to force you to go in a certain direction not good for you. It is hard to make a decision without God's guidance; it is difficult and confusing, but we can be sure that God wants us to find a fulfilling and rewarding path. We are free to make decisions, but each decision has consequences.

A youth who chooses a criminal path knows the consequences of that decision: jail or death. It's just a matter of time. A youth who chooses not to study in school reaps the consequences, that is, academic failure. Those who choose to engage in premarital sex know that there are consequences for that decision. The youth who chooses not to get job training faces the consequence of trying to find a job without a skill; that means unemployment.

Decisions come with consequences. Living without salvation has its consequence as well. We have been given the free rein to make decisions that impact our lives. We can make decisions to refrain or engage, but there are consequences. We can choose to sleep in one bed or many beds, but there are consequences. We can choose the high road or the low road in life, but there are consequences. When you are making a personal decision, get God's divine guidance and trust Him with your life.

The Church's Greatest Problems

Text

> I know thy works, and thy labour, and thy
> patience, and how thou canst not bear them
> which are evil: and thou hast tried them which
> say they are apostles, and are not, and hast found
> them liars. (Revelation 2:2)

Theme: The churches' greatest problem

We have so many church folks who seem to be just going through the motion as though they are just waiting for something catastrophic to happen. The joy has gone out of so many of our churches, and what the church needs lie in the realm of the intangibles. We are living in a time of need, but most of our needs are from above, and that is the Spirit of God. The churches' greatest problem is going around the problem and not facing it head-on.

Some folks seem to think that Christianity is a hitching post, but it is a guide post. We have some folks who mistake stagnation for harmony and activity for progress. It seems like our whole system of culture is a house divided against itself. We have too many divided churches saying they love the Lord, but their hearts are far from Him. The church suffers from a tragic dualism of glorifying man and degrading Him at the same time (two-faced people). The more the church improves its material conditions, sometimes the more it loses the power of God.

If God's power is not in the church, there is no peace. What we sometimes call peace is a pause between wars. We are having too much fighting in God's churches because we are going around the main problems and because we don't want to hurt someone's feelings. But what about God's feelings? The fruits of peace do not grow on trees of unrighteousness! But if the churches are going to have peace, they must invite the Holy Spirit into them.

We have some beautiful churches, but we must not let that beauty blind us of its sins. The greatest problem in our churches is that we have been going around the problem too long which has been causing the church to decline. We have too many churches that prepared reasons for revelation, theory to truth, culture to conversion, sociability to spirituality, and reformation to regeneration. We must stand up in God's church for the right thing even though trouble will come our way. But no cross, no crown.

We have too many churches that want to go through their resurrection without their crucifixion, but we have to go through our Gethsemane and Calvary. Christ faced the problems of the church, and they crucified Him on the cross. Jesus's heart, which had been so freely offered to men, was at last broken by human tormentors. The hands, which had touched the wasted bodies of lepers, were finally torn by unsterilized nails. Jesus, the man who had lifted burdens from the lives of others, eventually took the burdens of the world upon Himself. The best teacher the world has ever known was rejected and killed on the charge of blasphemy. He did this to face the greatest problem in the church—that is sin. He worked hard to redeem and transform His church.

The church did not invent the resurrection, but the resurrection created the church. Through God's power, cowards became heroes! The unstable became stable! He is our help in every sorrow. He is there in every weakness. He is there to give light in every dark valley. He is there to calm the storms of life. He is there to help the church to face the morrow. In our distress, He is there to give us peace in every difficult decision. He came for the first time to redeem the world. He will come the second time to judge the world.

The churches' greatest problem seems to be walking around sin and not facing it head-on. The Bible said, "Judgment will begin in the house of the Lord."

Underserved Salvation

Text

> Therefore it is of faith that it might be by
> grace; to the end that the promise might be sure
> to all the seed; not to that only which is of the law,
> but to that also which is of the faith of Abraham;
> who is the father of us all. (Romans 4:16)

Theme: Undeserved salvation

Abraham's faith was tested, but he had strong faith. Being a righteous person does not mean that trial is impossible or unnecessary. The greater the faith, the greater the trial. Faith has a way of shining through the dark clouds of doubts. Take away Abraham's trials, and where is his faith? Faith must be tried so that it may live. Faith, despite trials, glorifies God. Abraham's story is written in tears and blood, but how was God glorified by his trials of faith?

Abraham was called the father of the righteous because, out of his seed, God promised the savior of the world. He is the father of the righteous family, and not the disobedient father named Adam. Abraham's obedience of faith earned him honor. God called Abraham His friend; this was the greatest honor he could be given to a man.

God caused salvation to enter into this world through Abraham's seed to save this world. Isn't that good news? Psalm 121:1–2 says, "I will lift up mine eyes unto the hills from which cometh my help; my help cometh from the Lord which made heaven and earth." If you are seeking salvation, Matthew 11:15 says, "He that has ears to hear, let him hear." If you are seeking salvation, Romans 10:10 says, "For with the heart man believeth unto righteousness; and with the mouth, confession is made unto salvation." If you are seeking salvation, Philippians 2:5 says, "Let this mind be in you, which was also in Christ Jesus." Hebrews 12:1 says, "Let us lay aside every weight, and the sin which doth so easily beset us, and let us run with patience the race that is set before us." To receive salvation, we must let go of some of our extra baggage. They have a way of keeping us from reaching our spiritual destination.

God sent us the help we needed through the seed of Abraham—Jesus the Christ. This was the only man He could use to bring salvation to the world. He used Adam to start the human race. He used Abraham as the father of the righteous race, and through his seed came Jesus to bless the human race. God used Joseph to feed the race. He used Moses to lead the race. He used Sampson to be a fighter for the race. He used Solomon to inspire the race. He used David to be a singer for the race. God used Isaiah to visualize the race. He used Jeremiah to cry for the race. God used Daniel to pray for the race. He used John the Baptist to baptize the race. He used the man—Jesus—to die to bring salvation to the race.

Matthew 3:8 tells us that salvation brings about a change of mind. Romans 8:14–17 tells us that salvation brings about a change in family. Hebrews 10:14–16 tells us that salvation also brings about a change of behavior. You can't be the same when you receive salvation. Without salvation, we all will fall short of God's glory. God is absolutely pure and holy, and even one sin—just one—would be enough to keep you away from God's presence. It doesn't matter how good a person is; it wouldn't be good enough to get into God's presence without salvation.

What is salvation? It is deliverance from the power and effects of sin.

I Got This

Text

> Behold, God will not cast away a perfect man, neither will he help the evildoers: Till he fills thy mouth with laughing, and thy lips with rejoicing. They that hate thee shall be clothed with shame; and the dwelling place of the wicked shall come to naught. (Job 8:20–22)

Theme: I got this

Job's sufferings are intensified by three false friends, but God was letting Job know, "I got this." Job 4:8 tells us, "Even as I have seen, they that plow iniquity, and sow wickedness, reap the same." His first friend was Eliphaz, who bases his advice on personal experience. His second friend was Bildad, who bases his advice on tradition. The Bible spoke about the tradition that Bildad talked about: "For we are but of yesterday and know nothing, because our days upon earth are a shadow." His third friend was Zophar, who bases his advice on pure dogmatism. Job 11:6 says, "And that he would show thee the secrets of wisdom, that they are double to that which is! Know therefore that God exacteth of thee less than thine iniquity deserveth."

God is saying to us today, "Don't worry. I got this." After all Mr. Job had gone through, God was saying to him, "I got this, Job."

Don't worry or don't lose any sleep. God was not pleased with Job's friends calling him a hypocrite. It was wrong in God's sight. We sometimes sit in judgment and find faults that God can't find. In Job 1:8, the Lord told Satan that Job was a good man, and God went on to say, "He was perfect and an upright man." We sometimes need to sit down, shut up, get our lives straight with God, and stop trying to judge others and making a mess of other folks' lives.

God was letting Job know to not worry. He will deal with those who are trying to bring you down in His own time, but you don't have to do anything because He said, "I got this." Job's first trial was when his oxen and donkeys were stolen and his farmhands killed by a Sabean raid. His second trial was when his sheep and herdsmen were burned up by fire. His third was when his camels were stolen and his servants killed by a Chaldean raid. The fourth was when his sons and daughters perished in a mighty wind. Fifth was when he was struck with a terrible case of boils.

God let Job know, "I got this." He vindicated Job before the eyes of his three critical friends. God fully restored Job's health. Job was given double for his troubles. He was given more sons and daughters. He was given grandchildren and great-grandchildren. It was said, "God gave him an additional 140 years." How many of you have been told by God, "I got this," and you are trying to do it yourself?

God has the power to handle whatever problem you have. His power is deeper than hell, wider than the sea, and higher enough to kiss heaven. When God says, "I got this," it is in good hands. When we think about this country we live in, God is saying, "I got this."

When you think about Job's loss, God is saying, "I got this."

The Joy of Being a Doorkeeper

Text

> For a day in thy courts is better than a thou-
> sand. I had rather be a doorkeeper in the house
> of my God, than to dwell in the tents of wicked-
> ness. (Psalm 84:10)

> I was glad when they said unto me let us go
> into the house of the Lord. (Psalm 122:1)

Theme: The joy of being a doorkeeper

This Psalm tells us, "A day in thy courts is better than a thousand days anywhere else." The sons of Koran were doorkeepers. He
says, "He would rather have his job than be a rich man living far
from God." The psalmist says, "I have rather spend one day in God's
house than a thousand anywhere else." What a glorious Psalm this is,
and what a rebuke it is to many of us.

To be good ushers, you must first be born again and have love
for people. Ushers should carry a smile on their faces; a good usher
should be willing to make a contribution to man and God. An usher
can't party all night, walk the isles in God's church on Sunday morning, and say they love the Lord. Some folks love God with their lips,

but their hearts are far off. To be good ushers, you must have a little talk with Jesus before service because you will come face-to-face with all kinds of people. The Lord is saying to all of us, "Come unto me." He is saying, "Come all who have been rejected by the world. Come who are despair and who are lost. If you are worn, come. If you are weary, come." Come because there is joy in God's church, and His church cannot be duplicated.

God's church is too high for a man to reproduce. His church cannot be destroyed because the Bible says, "The gates of hell cannot prevail against it." Don't let Satan steal your joy of being a doorkeeper because there is joy in being a doorkeeper in God's church. God's church cannot be slowed down or stopped because it moves in eternity and not in time; eternity overruns time; time is no match for eternity.

God's church is here to stay. It is a joy to dwell in the house of the Lord. In Isaiah 6:1, Isaiah said, "I saw also the Lord sitting upon a throne high and lifted up, and his train filled the temple." It was in the temple where Isaiah saw the Lord.

He said, "Woe is me, for I am undone because I am a man of unclean lips and I dwell in the midst of a people of unclean lips." We must do as Isaiah did. We need to be cleaned up before going to work in God's house. We must not compromise with wrongdoings in God's church. To be a good usher, you have to stop listening to everything you hear; sometimes, we have to have an uncompromising attitude when it comes to wrongdoings in God's house.

You may dwell in God's house, but you are going to have trouble with Satan even in the church because he comes to church every Sunday. There is joy in God's house, but Satan tries to steal the joy out of God's church, but we should have the joy that can't be taken away. Satan is busy in God's churches because his time is running out.

In Hebrews, he was calling the king of death. Satan's job is to try to kill everything that is good, but God forbid. In John 12:31, John sees Him as the prince of this world. Ephesians 6:12 says he is the ruler of darkness. Revelation 20:10 says he is a deceiver. The scripture 1 Thessalonians 3:5 says he is the tempter. The scripture

2 Corinthians 11:14–15 says he is called the angel of light. Genesis 3:4–5 says he is called a murderer. He comes to kill and steal. He may come to church on Sunday morning, but don't let him steal your joy.

Be a proud doorkeeper in the house of the Lord. Be glad when they say unto you, "Let us go into the house of the Lord." There is joy in the house of the Lord because the Bible says, "A day in Thy courts is better than a thousand days anywhere else."

A Spiritual Checkup

Text

> O Lord, thou hast searched me, and know
> me. (Psalm 139:1)

Theme: A spiritual checkup

In Psalm 139:2–4,

> Thou knowest my down sitting and mine
> uprising, thou understandest my thought afar
> off. Thou compassest my path and my lying
> down, and art acquainted with all my ways. For
> there is not a word in my tongue, but lo, O Lord,
> thou knowest it altogether.

This Psalm speaks of the omniscience of God because He knows all things. God doesn't have to put you on an x-ray table to see through you. God is the greatest psychologist when you are having a problem; it is not necessary to climb on the psychiatrist's couch and tell him everything. He already knows our shortcomings. Some of us need to climb on the couch of the Lord Jesus and just tell Him everything in prayer. You might as well tell Him because He knows all about you anyway. The psychiatrist still won't know you even after you have told him everything you can think of, but God does. In Psalm 139:5, "Thou hast beset me behind and before, and laid thine hand upon me." In Psalm 139:6, "Such knowledge is too wonderful for me; it is nigh, I cannot attain unto it."

God can search a part of man that man can't see. While the body was being formed, God has the blueprint of His members before they come into existence. In Psalm 140:3, "They have sharpened their tongues like a serpent; adder's poison is under their lips." Doctors may not know how to fix the things that are needed because man's know-how is limited, but God is not. In Romans 11:33, "Oh the depth of the riches both of the wisdom and knowledge of God! How unsearchable is His judgment, and His ways past finding out!"

The Son is the radiance of God's glory and the exact representation of His being. Some theologians, such as Soren Kierkegaard and Karl Barth, reject all general or natural theology and claim that God can be known only as an act of faith. God is an all-knowing God. Two aspects of God's all knowledge are emphasized in the Scriptures. "Nothing happens without God." Man cannot hide either his actions or his thoughts from God. We need to also to search ourselves; we can't see what God can see, but we can do our best.

In this country, we need to search ourselves. We need to search ourselves when it comes to some folks who don't want to read the Bible in classrooms. We have too many church folks who the demon possessed, and they need to clean their acts up and stop playing with God. Proverbs 30:12 says, "There is a generation that is pure in their own eyes, and yet are not washed from their filthiness."

We need to ask God to teach us to search ourselves. There are people who think they are all right, but they are not sensitive to sin. In Romans 7:18, Paul, said, "For I know that in me that is, in my flesh, dwelleth no good thing." David went right down to the root of the matter. He confessed that he had a sin nature. When are some folks going to search themselves and confess their sins before it's too late?

In Psalm 139:1, "O Lord, thou has searched me, and know me." God has His own list.

Armed and Dangerous

Text

> For the word of God is quick, and pow-
> erful, and sharper than any two-edged sword,
> piercing even to the dividing asunder of soul and
> spirit, and of the joints and marrow, and is a dis-
> cerner of the thoughts and intents of the heart.
> (Hebrews 4:12)

Theme: Armed and dangerous

God's word is armed and dangerous to destroy the enemy. His
word is a destroyer. When it comes to the enemy, it is armed and
dangerous. God's word has the power to cut sins from left to right,
and it is here to stay when everything else passes away. God's word is
powerful. Jeremiah 23:29 says, "Is not my word like as a fire? saith
the Lord; and like a hammer that breaketh the rock in pieces?"

It is armed and dangerous. The word of God is living and active.
His word is sharper than any double-edged sword. It penetrates even
to dividing soul and spirit and joints and marrow; God's word judges
the thoughts and attitudes of the heart. It has been said, "Nothing
in all creation is unknown from God's sight." The word of God can
show us who we really are. We sometimes try to show folks a side

that isn't us. Do you know who you are? It is said, "The word is like an x-ray that has a way of revealing who we really are." God's word is armed and dangerous. It always gets in man or woman.

The only way we can overcome the flesh is through Jesus Christ. He said, "I am the way, the truth, and the life" (John 14:6). Paul said in Romans 7:18, "For I know that nothing good lives in me, this is, in my flesh." He also said, "For the desire to do what is good is within me, but there is no ability to do it." We sometimes don't allow the word of God to work in our lives. The word of God does not divide the soul from the spirit, but rather, it penetrates both the soul and the spirit.

Paul said in Romans 7:7, "Well then, am I suggesting that the law of God is sinful? Of course not! In fact, it was the law that showed me my sin. I would never have known that coveting is wrong if the law had not said, 'You must not covet.'"

"Let us know we can approach the throne of grace with confidence so that we may receive mercy and find grace to help us in our time of need." God's word is armed and dangerous to help you fight against sin. The word is armed and dangerous. God's word knows how to deal with Satan, but you don't. The word knows how to deal with suffering and storms of life. The word of God is armed and dangerous, and if we try to live without it, we will be like taking truth out of history and taking matter out of physics. We will be like a song without a singer and like taking the mind out of metaphysics. To try to live without the word is like taking numbers out of mathematics. To live without the word of God will be like a harp without a player.

This two-edged sword is the word of God, and it is armed and dangerous. It is the way to salvation, and it brings happiness to believers. It will make a dumb man wise, and if you live by it, you will overcome the world. It will give you the light of direction, comfort, and guidance. If you are traveling and seeking more light, He will be a map to guide you.

The two-edged sword is the living word; it is armed and dangerous. It is known to be the mind of God, men's compass, and the pilgrim's staff. It has been known as the Christian charter. We can be armed and dangerous if we stay in God's word. It is a powerful two-edged sword, cutting sin out of your life.

The Key to Drawing

Text

> And as Moses lifted up the serpent in the
> wilderness, even so must the Son of man be lifted
> up. (John 3:14)

Theme: The magnetic power of God

When we lift Jesus up, the power of His compassion and deity will draw all men to His bleeding side. True empowerment comes when men and women are inspired to step out and trust the power of God. We can't do anything without the power of the Holy Spirit directing and strengthening us. Some of the people were obedient, and they waited faithfully until, on the day of Pentecost, the power came. The people received an extraordinary gift of communication concerning God's word. We have some folks trying to do kingdom building without being empowered by God's Holy Spirit, and that is the reason some churches are headed in the wrong direction.

God took a handful of farmers, tax collectors, and fishermen and empowered them, and they turned the world upside down. We can't be in the power zone if we have not been empowered by the Holy Spirit. To lift Jesus, you need to be in God's power zone. If you are in God's power zone, you may stumble, but God will give you the power to lift His holy name.

If you get lost on your way, God will help you find your way. If you find yourself in the valley of despair, God will lift you to a mountaintop of hope. If you are walking in God's power zone, count it all joy when you enter into diverse temptations. You can't turn your enemy into friends until you get in God's power zone. Lift His name and not do evil for evil. We must lift His name; walk by faith and not by sight.

If you lift Jesus, He will give you that same power He used when He spat out the seven seas and decorated the night with the moon and stars! This is the same power that lifted Jesus from a borrowed grave. They put Jesus on the cross and lifted Him up. He was offered upon the cross to give us everlasting life. The world offers disturbance, but the cross offers us peace of mind. The world offers defilement, but the cross offers purity of spirit. The world offers hate, but the cross offers uncorrupted love. The world offers darkness, but the cross offers us light and joy forevermore. This world offers weakness, but the cross offers divine strength.

If you lift Jesus, He will dissolve your doubt. He will satisfy your longings. He will dry your tears. Just lift Jesus and stay anchored in His love. This country needs to lift Jesus because we have been blind trying to lead the blind. We have too many folks who are financially lame, but you must keep lifting Jesus. We have too many folks whose hopes are paralyzed, but they keep lifting Jesus. He has given us the key to drawing men and women to His kingdom. Jesus is that master key.

In Isaiah 22:22, "And the key of the house of David will I lay upon his shoulder; so he shall open, and none shall shut; and he shall shut and none shall open." In Matthew 16:19, Jesus gave Peter the keys to the kingdom so that he could draw men and women to the kingdom. "Whosesoever sins ye remit, they are remitted unto them; and whosoever sins ye remit, they are retained" (John 20:23).

In Luke 11:52, "Woe unto you lawyers: for ye have taken away the key of knowledge: ye entered not in your selves, and them that were entering in were hindered." In 2 Thessalonians 3:14, "And if any man obey not our word by this epistle note that man, and have no company with him, that he may be ashamed."

The Model Servant

Text

As free, and not using your liberty for a cloak of maliciousness, but as the servants of God. Honor all men. Love the brotherhood. Fear God. Honor the king. Servants, be subject to your masters with all fear; not only to the good and gentle, but also to the forward. (1 Peter 2:16–18)

Theme: A model servant

The primary model for all Christians is Jesus Christ Himself. He "left us an example, so that we would follow in His footstep." Jesus came to serve. He said, "The son of man didn't come to be served; he came to give his life to redeem the lost" (Mark 10:45). Jesus dramatically illustrated His servant lifestyle for His disciples. Jesus wanted His servant to learn an unmistakable basic lesson of servanthood. The terms "the servant of the Lord," "my servant," or "His servant" were the pronouns (referring to God) are applied to many leaders of God's people. Moses was called servant over thirty times. David was called over seventy times and, to Israel as a nation, a number of times.

In contrast, God told Israel not to fear. "But you, Israel, my servant, Jacob whom I have chosen, descendant of Abraham my friend, you are my servant, I have chosen you and not rejected you" (Isaiah 41:8). Isaiah 42 gives a remarkable picture of the ideal servant to the Lord and the great work that God intends him to accomplish. In Acts 3:13, "In the resurrection and ascension, God glorified Jesus the servant."

The Greek word for *servant* appears through the KJV and translates as *son*. In Acts 4:29–30, "This led the early church to pray that as God's servant they would speak with boldness and perform miracles through the name of the Model servant Jesus Christ." In Luke 4:18–19, Jesus saw His mission as that of the servant.

Can Anything Good Come Out of Suffering?

Text

> What if God, willing to show his wrath, and to make his power known, endured with much longsuffering the vessels of wrath fitted to destruction. (Romans 9:22)

Theme: Can anything good come out of suffering?

It has been said, "All suffering is due to sin as introduced by Adam." The Bible says that creation, in the beginning, was made good and free from sin and pain. Something happened. When sin entered, suffering also entered in the form of conflict, pain, and corruption. And that brought about death. Christ came to deliver mankind from sin and corruption, but it caused Him to suffer. Satan is regarded as having the power to make man suffer. That power is only in the hands of God. It is God who controls and allows suffering because of sin. God's power is the only power that can change the evil in this universe. Instead, He tolerates it and uses it to His advantage. God uses it to punish individuals and nations.

Christians experience suffering, troubles, and persecutions that are part of God's way of giving to His own the way to grow into powerful Christians. The miracles Jesus performed and His own resurrection proved that He has all power. Jesus could have healed Lazarus as easily as by raising him from the dead. Jesus sometimes chooses not to use His power on certain things.

Jesus, on the other hand, could have prevented Herod from arresting, imprisoning, and killing John the Baptist, but He chose not to do so. Jesus knew that God would be somewhat glorified by John's death than by letting him live. Herod was not in charge of John's death, but he was only performing what God permitted him to do (Mark 1:14). It was power given from God's hand to Herod to take a life.

The Bible tells us that all suffering, sickness, and death are because of what happened in the beginning—the sins of Adam. Some of God's greatest saints suffered more than some sinners to demonstrate God's sufficiency through their breaking the necessary consequences of sinful humanity.

Claim It and Gain It

Text

> Therefore I say unto you, what things so
> ever ye desire, when ye pray, believe that ye receive
> them, and ye shall have them. (Mark 11:24)

Theme: To gain it, you must claim it

When you gain something, it means it is in your possession. To claim something is a demand for something due, believed to be, and a right to something. Mark 11:24 gives us the right to possess what we ask for in faith. This text tells us to have faith in God and to ask in faith. This does not give you the ability to satisfy your own selfish desires but to have faith in God that His will might be done in your life.

John 14:12–14 says,

> I tell you the truth, anyone who has faith
> in me will do what I have been doing. He will
> do even greater things than these, because I am
> going to the Father. He says, And I will do what-
> ever you ask in my name, so that the Son brings

glory to the Father. You may ask me for anything in my name, and I will do it.

Isaiah 41:17 says,

> The poor and needy search for water, but there is none; their tongues are parched with thirst. But I the Lord will answer them; I, the God of Israel, will not forsake them.

Mark 11:24 talks about prayer: The condition to prayer is expectancy. A man must believe and expect the answer to his prayer. He must be confident and assured and must anticipate and look for the answer (Matthew 21:22). The exact words of Jesus's promises are interesting. Let us glance at the verse Mark 11:22–23. Expectancy involves all of man's being: the spirit of expectancy.

"Faith in prayer": The first condition to prayer is faith in God. The object of faith is God Himself. The critical words are *"in God."* Jesus did not say, "Have faith," but "Have faith in God." Faith has to have an object. "In God" is where one is to place his faith. Faith has no value by itself; only the object, which is God, has the value.

The Bible never says, "To have faith in faith," but you must have it in God. Man's faith is not going to move the mountain; it is the object of faith, which is God, that the mountain will be moved. Faith requires us to know the object. The more one knows the object of faith, the more one believes in the object (Hebrews 11:6).

God is generous: He gives everything needed. He is patient, and He expects payment; He is patient, and He sends messengers to receive payment. God is love; He sends His very own Son to the world to pay for man's sins. God is just; He shall come to destroy evil keepers. In 1 Corinthians 12:4–11, God gives His followers the gift, the equipment they need to carry out their tasks on earth. In Matthew 6:25–34, God gives His followers the assurance and security of His care.

To "claim it and gain it," you must have faith in God. Faith is the beginning of a triumphant life. Knowledge is faith consummation. Faith reveals the way, but knowledge is the goal. Faith walks in darkness but believes, and knowledge acts in light. Faith is the substance of things hoped for, but knowledge is the substance of things possessed. Without faith, there will be no knowledge; when knowledge is acquired, the work of faith is finished. God has a blessing for you, but you must claim it to gain it and have faith.

Counterfeit Christians

Text

> Ye shall know them by their fruits. Do men
> gather grapes of thorns, or figs of thistles? Even
> so every good tree bringeth forth good fruit; but
> a corrupt tree bringeth forth evil fruit. (Matthew
> 7:16–18)

Theme: Counterfeit Christians

How can we recognize a counterfeit Christian? They are recognized by their fruits. We have too many folks running around talking about how they love Jesus, but they are holding out on Jesus and not even giving it a thought. We are following the wrong group of Christians. There are two kinds of Christians: the counterfeit and the real Christian. The counterfeit Christians are not for the things of God's kingdom; they fight against everything of God. You have to be very careful because you can easily be deceived.

The Bible said, "Take heed that no man deceive you." The counterfeit Christians are going to keep conflicts among God's people because this is the sign of the end. We are approaching the end of time; this old world is going into labor, and we all can feel the pain. We can see in this world of ours that the birth pains are getting stronger, and time is getting closer. We can tell by all these counterfeit Christians that the end time is coming to a climax.

It seems like things are not getting any better, but they seem to be getting worse. I believe God is getting ready to give birth to a new-world order. God's people are going to be hated by those counterfeit Christians for His name's sake. God's representatives are going to face persecution and be hated, and if you are getting some feedback, don't worry; just be happy you are God's representative.

We see some so-called Christians who just won't work together. Rather than working together, they seem to be happier divided, and that breaks the heart of God. It pleases God when He sees His people characterized with love. We have too many counterfeit Christians or people in our churches and in politics, trying to control our economic system. We have counterfeit people who are able to fool people because the people listen to them. We saw that happen in the November election. They are listening to the counterfeit leaders. We don't know what the future holds unless God speaks it to our hearts. We have too many counterfeit people saying they are speaking what God told them, but I don't believe God had anything to do with it.

We have too many prophets and not enough winning souls for Jesus. We need to get our heads out of the clouds of prophecy and put them on the pavement of winning souls for Jesus. We are listening to many counterfeit prophets; we need to listen to the message of Jesus Christ. We need to warn people to flee from the wrath to come and be saved.

A real Christian has been tried in the fire of life. Tears and sadness may come, but joy will come in the morning. A real Christian may be tried, but despite the hopeless situation, God is able to deliver His people. If you are a real Christian, you will be able to walk a different walk filled with anticipation. A real Christian will never give up hope; they may endure many rising and falling, but God will never abandon or forsake them. God's people will sing a new song to the counterfeit Christian: They will declare, "We are on the battlefield for our Lord. We promise Him that we would serve Him till we die. We are on the battlefield for our Lord."

Don't Be a Dropout

Text

> From that time many of his disciples went back, and walked no more with him. Then said, Jesus unto the twelve, will ye also go away? Then Simon Peter answered him, Lord, to whom shall we go? Thou hast the words of eternal life. (John 6:66–68)

Theme: Don't be a dropout"

Dropping out has a way of costing a person a lifetime; it cost Judas Iscariot eternal life. Dropping out costs a price. Judas Iscariot didn't graduate from the school of eternal life because he dropped out. I extend my congratulations for your hard work and for completing the requirements to finish school. Thank God you were not a dropout. I tried hard for the summa cum laude, but I was blessed with a magna cum laude, but I just thank God I made it, and I didn't drop out. I congratulate the parents for their determination and the students for not dropping out but finishing the difficult task.

We look at this as a day of satisfaction and making it to the finishing line; you can't make it to the finishing line by dropping out. If we want to do beautiful things, we must not be a dropout. If Aristotle had been a dropout, he would not be speaking to us concerning the works of art. He said, "A work of art can also give pleasure, because it is beautiful…The beauty of a work of art, lies in unity, if you want to make it to the finish line you must keep in unity with God, and don't be a dropout."

If Immanuel Kant had dropped out of school, he wouldn't be telling us there is more to reality than the world of nature we see, hear, touch, and perceive with our senses. If all the math teachers had dropped out of school, we wouldn't know how to count from one to five. The zero is a placeholder, but it shows us how much the other numerals stand for in a number. If the zero is put into the right place, it can make a difference. You can take the zero and put it behind a one, and it will make a difference. It will give you ten.

Some people may look at you like a zero, but if you stay in school and put yourself in the right place, you can be like the zero and be able to make a difference in life. If the philosophers had dropped out of school, we wouldn't have anyone telling us about the outer limits of life and the hidden essence of being alive.

Don't walk away from the significant things in life (John 6:66–68).

Doubt versus Hope

Text

> Be of good courage, and he will strengthen your heart, all ye that hope in the Lord. (Psalm 31:24)

> Our soul waiteth for the Lord: he is our help and our shield. (Psalm 33:20)

Theme: Doubt versus hope

God's word gives us hope for tomorrow; the word of God is the unsearchable riches and a treasure house of divine grace. "Thus signs of hope outshines all previous disasters." Hope will give you the faith to believe that the creation will be in full bloom, and the rains will fall again. We must put our trust in the Lord. The threshing floors will be full of grain, and the vats will overflow with oil and wine; the world needs a spectacular spiritual renewal experience; God is still offering hope to His people. We need to have faith and lay hold of God's promise of hope.

What is hope? It is a desire accompanied by expectation. What is faith? It is fidelity to one's promise and sincerity of intentions. Also, it is the sustaining of things hoped for and evidence of things not seen. We need to believe, trust, and be loyal to the Lord who is able to give us hope in times of need. If we trust God, He will never fail us—the one in who you can put confidence. We can put all our trust in God, and He will never fail us.

We are living in a time we don't know what to expect these days, but God is our hope in times of need. We are living in a time of depersonalizing influences and dehumanizing tactics, and in this technology age, it seems like computers are taking over the world. In this highly scientific age, when it seems like machines are given more importance than man, God has given mankind hope from Genesis through Revelation.

In Genesis 2:17, we are told that "man shall surely die," but Revelation 21:4 says, "There will be no more death." In Genesis 2:21, "The first bride was taken from the wounded side of the first Adam." In Revelation 21:9, "The second bride, which is the Church, is taken from His wounded side, and He will call the second Adam; which is Jesus Christ."

In Genesis, the first marriage was performed by God in the presence of the angels. In Revelation 19:9, the last marriage will be performed by God in the presence of redeemed saints. There is hope in the Lord. In Genesis 3:14–19, a fourfold curse is pronounced. In Revelation 22:3, "There will be no more curse." In Genesis 3:22–24, The first Adam was defeated by Satan, but there was hope in Jesus Christ. In Revelation 19:21 and 20:10, the second Adam is victorious; he is Jesus Christ.

All our help comes from the Lord. In Genesis 3:21, we read of the sacrifice of the first lamb. In Revelation 14:1, we see the lamb standing victorious on Mount Zion. If your hope is in Jesus, you can always stand on the promises of the Lord. Standing on the promises of Christ my king; stand on the promises of the Lord. Through eternal ages, let His praises ring; stand on the promises of the Lord. Glory in the highest. I will shout and sing, standing on the promises of the Lord.

When you put your hope in Jesus and not in doubt, you can stand on that promise that will not fail. When the howling storms of doubt and fear assail you, you can stand on the promises of the

Lord. There is hope in Jesus: What can wash away our sin? Nothing but the blood of Jesus. What can make us whole again? Nothing but the blood of Jesus.

Oh, precious is the flow that makes us white as snow—nothing but the blood of Jesus. No other fount I know, nothing, but the blood of Jesus. Time is filled with swift transitions. Naught of earth unmoved can stand. Build your hope on things eternal. Hold to God's unchanging hand.

Farsighted Christians

Text

> The light of the body is the eye: if therefore
> thine eye be single, thy whole body shall be full
> of light. But if thane eye be evil, thy whole body
> shall be full of darkness. If therefore the light that
> is in thee be darkness, how great is that darkness!
> (Matthew 6:22–23)

Theme: Farsighted Christians

Farsighted Christians are folks in the church who are able to see the goal but can't see how to deal with the daily flow of time, talents, and resources to achieve the goal. We have folks who are able to see the goal but can't put it into action. It is bad when God gives a person far-sight to see a problem and that person doesn't care enough to do anything about it. We have too many Christians who have blurry eyesight; no matter how you try to show them the right way, they can't see the truth.

It is said, "Even if we keep our objective in sight but fail to con-centrate our energies, our lives still become a blur failure." We have some nearsighted so-called Christians who can't see things unless they are close-up; they have no far sight for tomorrow. We have some people who spend everything they have in one day; they don't believe in trying to achieve long-term goals. They are not like the ants that follow the general creed that they should eat, drink, and be merry, for tomorrow may never come. The ants prepare for tomorrow.

We must stay focused and keep our eyes on the mark of the high calling of Jesus Christ. We have some so-called Christians who suffer from spiritual stigmatism; they see things but not very clearly. We have folks who can see things when it comes to someone else's actions, but they can't see anything they do.

We need to keep our eyes on Jesus because He is Jehovah-Rapha. He has the power to heal and set free. He is Jehovah-Shalom: He is a storm calmer. He is Jehovah-Nissi: He is victory over our adversities. God will give you victory. If we put our trust in Jesus: His promises will never fail us. His Glory will never fade away. His joy will never come to an end. His blessings will never stop coming. His foundation is unshakable and we are our heavenly Father's children, and he knows just how much we can bear! He is able to deal with us when we are spiritually Far Sighted, and Near Sighted in our ways of life.

Rev. Dr. B. W. Freeman

ABOUT THE AUTHOR

Rev. Dr. Burness W. Freeman was born on March 23, 1941, in Chesterfield County, South Carolina.

God blessed him to be a pastor of seven churches. He always wanted to help orchestrate God's word to penetrate the hearts of mankind.

People need to teach mankind about the written word and the living word that teaches us to accept salvation.

Education

- Marlboro County High School, Bennettsville, South Carolina—diploma
- Shaw University, Bachelor of Arts in Religion and Philosophy—degree
- Hampton University Minister Conference, Hampton Virginia
- Wachovia Banking School, Florence, South Carolina
- The Professional Institute of Development for Chaplain, at the National Baptist Congress at Huston, Texas—diploma
- American Baptist College, National Baptist congress of Christian Education,—Diploma
- Masters of Divinity, LH Divinity Seminary at Beebe, Arkansas

- Tri-County Bible College and Seminary, Doctrine of Pastoral Minster—degree
- Rev. Dr. B. W. Freeman was awarded an honorary doctrine from Try-County Bible College & Seminary.
- Rev. Dr. B.W. Freeman received an honorary doctrine degree from the Baptist Educational and Missionary Convention of South Carolina at Morris College in Sumter, South Carolina, in September 2018.

Professional Accomplishments

- President of Morris College Cheraw's Alumni Chapter until July 17, 2022
- Former Moderator of the St. Paul Union, Chesterfield County, South Carolina
- Former President of the Bright Light Missionary and Education Convention Kershaw County, South Carolina
- Vice Moderator of the Educational and Building Union, Chesterfield County, South Carolina
- Dr. B.W. Freeman was awarded the Pastoral Ministry Award for 50 years or more in pastoral ministry, during the 137th annual session of the National Baptist Convention, USA, Inc. on September 7, 2017